NOTES ON GREEK SCULPTURE

NOTES ON GREEK SCULPTURE

I. THE CONSTANTINOPLE PENTATHLETE AND EARLY ATHLETE STATUES · II. A MARBLE DRAPED FEMALE FIGURE IN BURLINGTON HOUSE

by

SIR CHARLES WALSTON (WALDSTEIN)

LITT.D., PH.D.

Fellow of King's College, Cambridge; Sometime Reader in Classical Archaeology and Slade Professor of Fine Art, Director of the Fitzwilliam Museum, Cambridge; Director of the American School of Archaeology, Athens; author of *Essays on the Art of Pheidias*—*The Argive Heraeum*—*Herculaneum, Past, Present and Future* (with L. Shoobridge)—*Greek Sculpture and Modern Art*, etc.

CAMBRIDGE

AT THE UNIVERSITY PRESS

MCMXXVII

CAMBRIDGE
UNIVERSITY PRESS

University Printing House, Cambridge CB2 8BS, United Kingdom

Published in the United States of America by Cambridge University Press, New York

Cambridge University Press is part of the University of Cambridge.

It furthers the University's mission by disseminating knowledge in the pursuit of education, learning and research at the highest international levels of excellence.

www.cambridge.org
Information on this title: www.cambridge.org/9781107663626

First published 1927
First paperback edition 2014

A catalogue record for this publication is available from the British Library

ISBN 978-1-107-66362-6 Paperback

PREFACE

THE following "Notes" were read at the meeting of the Society for the Promotion of Hellenic Studies at Burlington House on February 8 of this year. As, however, owing to congestion of material, they cannot appear in the *Journal of Hellenic Studies* before next September and it is desirable that the problems here dealt with should be presented to my colleagues as soon as possible, the present form of special and preliminary publication has been adopted, so that, e.g., the identification of the Burlington House Marble should be finally effected. My suggestion that the marble torso formed part of the Nereid-monument of Xanthus is, of course, merely hypothetical. The microscopic examination of the marbles themselves, kindly undertaken by Dr H. H. Thomas, of the Geological Survey, to which Dr Prior, of the Natural History Museum, also gave the material in his Museum and his experience, is not finally conclusive. For Dr Thomas's report confirms—what I had before learnt from colleagues—that it is often difficult to distinguish *microscopically* between Pentelic and Parian marbles and even between different parts of the same quarry. *Macroscopically*, however, we are able generally to determine such differences in ancient statues the surface of which has remained intact. But Dr Thomas's report makes it clear that the marble is neither Italian (Carrara) nor modern.

I have omitted from this publication the third Note as read. It dealt with "Works of Doubtful Antiquity." I felt that, since the death of Professor Furtwängler (to whom Archaeology owes a great debt), it is desirable not to revive former controversies. This is especially the case since I feel convinced that he would himself have repudiated the small bronze head from the Somzée Collection of Brussels of which, together with similar modern reductions of ancient larger heads, I actually possess modern replicas. The same applies to the terracotta Head of Zeus (now in the Museum of Frankfurt-a.-M.) which, at the Burlington Fine Art Club's exhibition of 1903, Furtwängler pronounced as Attic work of the fifth century B.C. of the school of Phidias, if not by the great sculptor himself. Dr J. Sieveking has since then (*Münchener Jahrbuch der bildenden*

Kunst, 1911, I) informed us that Furtwängler accepted his own view that the head belonged to the Roman period.

Since these Notes were written, Mr A. W. Lawrence has published an article on "*The Date of the Nike of Samothrace*" (*J.H.S.* XLVI, Part II, 1926; issued January 22, 1927). His arguments are interesting and, in part, convincing. The three torsos on Pl. XI show similarities in style and technique to our Burlington House torso. But he does not solve the important and difficult problem as to the treatment of drapery in the second half of the fifth century B.C., from the female figures in the pediments and frieze of the Parthenon, the sculptures of Phigalia, the Argive Heraeum, the Erechtheum, the temple of Nike Apteros and the Nereid-monument of Xanthus down to the work of Thrasymedes at Epidaurus in the fourth century B.C.

I must thank Mr C. D. Bicknell for having kindly seen this manuscript through the press.

C. W.

NEWTON HALL, NEWTON,
CAMBRIDGE

February 16, 1927.

Note. Since the above was written Sir Charles Walston has passed away. He was unable to correct the proofs, and my thanks are due to his old friend and colleague, Sir Cecil Harcourt Smith, formerly Director of the British School in Athens and Director of the Victoria and Albert Museum, for having done so.

F. W.

April, 1927.

LIST OF ILLUSTRATIONS

PLATE I

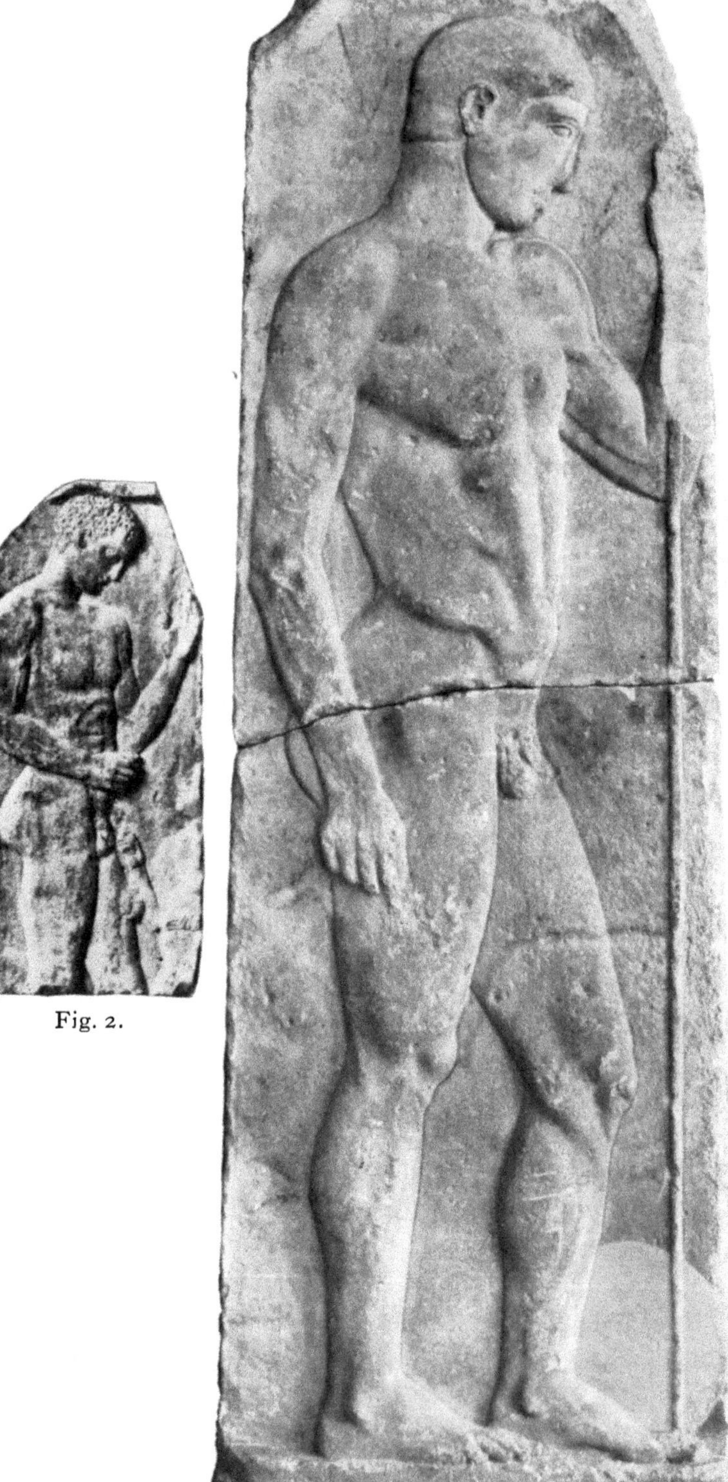

Fig. 2.

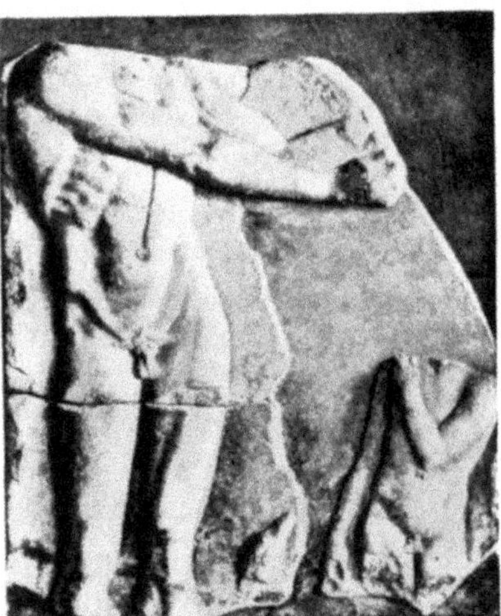

Fig. 3.

Fig. 1.

NOTES ON GREEK SCULPTURE

I

THE CONSTANTINOPLE PENTATHLETE AND EARLY ATHLETE STATUES

THE sepulchral marble slab, found on the Island of Nisyros in November 1900 (Pl. I, fig. 1), presents in flat relief the figure of a nude athlete, with a discus at his feet, resting on a spear held in the left hand. It figures in the Museum of Constantinople as No. 11 (1142), *Stèle funéraire d'un discobole*, and is fully described in vol. 1, p. 73 seq., of the excellent Catalogue of the Sculptures in that Museum by Dr G. Mendel, in which practically the whole of the literature pertaining to it is also given on p. 76[1].

The first reason which prompts the publication of this note is, that the figure of an athlete on this interesting monument ought in the future to be called, not that of a diskobolos, but of a pentathlete; for such it undoubtedly represents. The sculptors' presentation, whether in the round or in relief, of victors, beyond all doubt, in the pentathlon (however frequent the presentation of these five games together are on vases) has hitherto been unknown to me, in so far as more than one of the five games are shown in one work. In the relief we are considering we have the clear indication that the athlete was victorious in at least two of the field games, constituting the five games of the pentathlon, which, as has been admitted, served to encourage the all-round athlete in contradistinction to the specialised contests which tended to develop and to encourage skill as well as strength in one form of athletic activity.

[1] Among the various articles there referred to (which I have consulted as far as they were accessible), I would single out that of S. Reinach (*Revue Archéol.* 1901, pp. 158 seq. Pl. XV), who accords full artistic appreciation to this slab, notes an interesting series of such reliefs, and, in agreement with Furtwängler, points out its relationship to the Olympia pediments. Cf. also Lechat, *Revue des Études Grecques*, XIV (1901), pp. 420 seq.

We may perhaps except the pankration, which combined boxing with wrestling, but did not include running, jumping and throwing the discus and the spear, and thus did not develop fleetness and skill in throwing, which the pentathlon supplied.

I do not propose here to enter upon the complicated question of the relationship and sequence of the five contests in the pentathlon[1], and still less upon the problem of judging and assigning the prize for the five games as a whole. Even if I were more competent to do this, the matter has already been discussed by Mr E. Norman Gardiner and, latterly, by Capt. Lauri Pihkala in the *Journal of Hellenic Studies*[2]. The main point to which I wish to draw attention is the fact that the sculptor's task in commemorating the victory of a pent-athlete was fraught with many difficulties. Probably the discus as an attribute, and the various phases of throwing it, formed the most popular and easily expressible subject to commemorate the victory in the whole of the pentathlon. Running presented an extremely difficult task to the sculptor, though we can understand how the peculiar artistic character and achievement of Myron, with precocious realism presenting complex and momentary action, made it possible for him to produce the striking statue of Ladas[3] at the supreme final moment of winning his race, which inspired the epigrammatist to exclaim that Ladas, "with the last gasp of exhausted breath, seems to reach forward to snatch the victor's wreath." It was formerly thought that the two statues of nude youths bending forward with outstretched arms represented runners; though the view now held is that they represented opponents in a wrestling match about to secure a favourable first grip. To represent a wrestler in a single statue or a single figure in relief with undoubted clearness was also beyond the reach of the sculptor, especially in the early centuries of Greek art. Nor did the *halteres*, especially when actually used in moments of jumping, attract the sculptor to plastic presentation, however adequately such moments could be depicted upon painted vases.

There thus only remained the discus and the spear (ἀκόντιον) to indicate in a nude athlete these two field-games respectively;

[1] Besides the older classic treatise of J. H. Krause (*Gymnastik und Agonistik*), I must refer the reader to E. Norman Gardiner's *Greek Athletic Sports and Festivals* (and his articles in the *J.H.S.*).

[2] Vol. XLV (1925), pp. 132 seq.

[3] Overbeck, *Schriftquellen*, 542, Anthol. Gr. IV, 185, 318 (Planud. IV, 54).

while, when combined in one work of sculpture, as is the case in this Constantinople slab, the athlete is clearly shown as a competitor and victor in the pentathlon. It is not impossible that the nude figures with a spear and without armour were victors in these contests and possibly were pentathletes; and it is therefore not impossible that the famous statue of the Doryphoros of Polykleitos and kindred works served the same purpose. But our slab clearly combines the two contests of the pentathlon, in which, we may assume, the youth was victorious. Should, owing to a tie, the third or decisive contest of wrestling have been introduced, it seems probable, from the indication of all-round bodily strength of the youth here presented, that he may have been victorious in this third contest of wrestling as well. Mr E. Norman Gardiner seems to have accepted the suggestion that the *τριασμός* thus served to indicate the final test of wrestling to decide between those who had tied in the pentathlon.

Dr Mendel has shown how the slab was surmounted by a palmette and how, in his opinion, the background was coloured so as to bring the flat relief-work into clear prominence; while no doubt the discus (in some lights hardly visible) was clearly presented through the difference of colour between it and the background. In our photograph such device was necessarily used.

There can, to my mind, also be hardly any doubt that the very slightly roughened hair, which is here not indicated in texture and almost looks like a cap, was accentuated by means of colour, as, e.g., we find must have been the case in some of the heads from the pediments of the Temple of Zeus at Olympia. I have elsewhere[1] dwelt upon the close relationship between painted and sculptured marble slabs and shall presently dwell upon the significance of this fact in the chronological development of such works of sculpture.

The date which Dr Mendel and others assign to this work is *circ.* 470 B.C.; while S. Reinach gives 470 to 460 B.C. I am, on the whole, in agreement with this, though I prefer a slightly later date. As so dated it is of importance in showing the evolution of relief technique in the transitional period of Greek art down to the year 450 B.C., as well as in the treatment, especially of the head and the hair, in early athlete statues.

[1] *Alcamenes, etc.*, p. 61, n. 1.

When now we consider the artistic character of this relief, and through it the date to be assigned to it, we can, roughly speaking, with some certainty, assign to it a date posterior to the Persian War; but, for reasons which will become evident, I am inclined to fix this date five or even ten years later than that given by Dr Mendel in his Catalogue (namely, 470 B.C.). It would thus have been produced from 465/455 B.C., or even from 460/450 B.C.

The composition of the figure standing erect, while at the same time leaning on the spear held in the left hand, is thoroughly natural and free from any restraint and shows exquisite skill in the technique of flat relief-work. The figure is resting upon the right leg (*Standbein*), the knee of which is pressed backward; while the left leg (*Spielbein*) is advanced, though the foot is firmly planted on the ground, but is flexed at the knee. Were it not for the resting of the upper part of the body on the spear held in the left hand, the figure might be seen in complete profile, as the legs and head are treated. But the raising of the left arm and shoulder and the throwing of the weight of the body as regards the upper part upon the extended left arm, necessitates a forward turn of the body from the waist upwards and thus shows this upper part one-quarter towards the spectator's right, with a corresponding turn towards the frontal view in the torso. This complex position is indicated with great skill on the part of the sculptor, necessitating a difference in the relaxed position of the right shoulder with the arm naturally hanging by the side, while his left shoulder with the upturned forearm necessitates a swelling and rise of the shoulder muscle and corresponding turn towards the front of this part of the body. Thus, from the lowest part of the waist upwards to the neck, the torso itself is gradually turned from the profile view slightly towards the frontal view. The skill thus shown in composition by the sculptor is greatly increased when we consider the very low and flat relief of this complex action shown in the nude body and retained in its lowness throughout the whole of the slab, the outline of the whole figure, from top to bottom, having been carefully sunk into the background. This masterly treatment in low relief technique and composition is also shown in the details of the modelling of sinews and muscles, pectoral, shoulders and arms, and even in the indication of veins, as is shown in the vein running along the biceps to the inside of the elbow of the right arm. We are almost reminded of the passage referring to the advance made in sculpture by Pythagoras, *nervos et venas expressit*[1].

This consistent and masterly treatment may be contrasted with two reliefs of a later date which might almost be considered to be inferior variants of the original type by a true master fixed in this earlier relief from Nisyros. I have elsewhere[2] shown how, in the well-known Naples relief, the lower part of the leg presents the full frontal view, while from the knee upwards we have the profile view. Another slab (Pl. I, fig. 2) (of exceptional interest, because of the two drawings identified with it and published by Amelung[3]), though, from the treatment of the head, it must be at least ten to fifteen years later than our relief, shows awkwardly the complete profile view from the waist downwards, whereas the torso above it is in pronounced two-thirds frontal view. The same discrepancy applies to another sepulchral slab from Delphi[4] (Pl. I, fig. 3). In this we also have the frontal view in the lower part of the body from the waist downwards, while a twist to the left gives a two-thirds frontal view and even shows the sides of the ribs on the left side[5].

Now, the attitude of the pentathlete of the Nisyros slab, with both feet firmly planted on the ground, with the short and rather thick legs and protruding buttocks, is of that severer order which points to the earlier transitional period and corresponds to some degree to the profile view of the Choiseul-Gouffier "Apollo," with whom the pentathlete has, in other respects as well, some analogies; but it certainly differs from this statue as regards the head, as well

[1] Plin. *N.H.* xxxiv, 11, *hic primus nervos et venas expressit capillumque diligentius.* I cannot here enter into the complicated question of the treatment of the hair by Pythagoras.

[2] *Alcamenes, etc.*, p. 63.

[3] *Jahrb. d. Arch. Inst.* xviii (1903), pp. 109 seq., Pl. VIII, figs. 1 and 2; first discovered by Marucchi in Rome in the Church of *San Lorenzo in foro piscium* and published in the *Atti della Pontificia Accademia romana di archeologia*, 1902, pp. 473 seq., Pl. II; and, with other drawings, by S. Reinach, *L'Album de Pierre Jacques, sculpteur de Reims*, Paris, 1902.

[4] Homolle, *Centenaire de la société nationale des antiquaires de France* (1804–1904), p. 217, Pl. XVI; Benndorf, *Forschungen in Ephesos*, 1, 190 6, p. 197, Fig. 146; Poulsen, *Delphi* (translated by Richards and P. Gardner), p. 236, Fig. 107.

[5] There are later slabs of the same kind, e.g. Thespian Stelæ (publ. by Rodenwald, *Thespische Reliefs, Jahrb.* xxviii (1913), pp. 30 seq.). One youth (Pl. XXV) is shown completely in profile, another in frontal view.

as from the head of Harmodios at Naples[1], the Roman slab, as well as the Delphi slab (just mentioned) and the head of the Diskobolos of Myron[2].

In the case of our pentathlete the hair is treated as if a cap were tightly drawn over the top of the head[3]; but it certainly is left in the marble treatment slightly roughened and was probably coloured, as, in all probability, the background and the discus were coloured. Thus, polychromy was called in to indicate the hair in this relief.

I have elsewhere[4] drawn attention to the fact that, as in the case of the Lyseas stele[5], the representation on a flat marble slab was entirely painted on the surface, so, in other slabs and marble statues as well, the profuse pictorial ornamentation found on the softer stone in the pre-Persian Attic pedimental figures, was continued for some time. It was, no doubt, owing to the development of marble technique that the details, such as hair, were actually indicated by rise and fall of strands and curls in modelling and carving. Towards the middle of the fifth century B.C. and certainly with Myron's Diskobolos (Fig. 4), the sculptor no longer depended upon assistance from the painter. But in the transitional period, from *circ.* 470/450 B.C., there was, as it were, a struggle between the two methods, until the sculptor's modelling predominated. We thus have, in the pediments from the Temple of Zeus at Olympia, side by side, the two methods of indication of hair by colour on a flat surface, as well as modelled plastic indication of the texture of hair.

Our relief from Nisyros thus indicates this struggle, while still applying the earlier polychrome treatment to the hair. I should thus be inclined to date it about the year 465 to 455 B.C. But we must also note the fact that, in any case, the hair was represented as short. Here, again, the transitional period down to the Diskobolos of Myron represents this struggle in transition between the short and long haired athlete and ephebos.

[1] Studniczka, *Zum Delphischen Wagenlenker* (*Jahrb. d. Arch. Inst.* XXII, 1907, pp. 133 seq., Beilage to p. 137).

[2] The composite restoration of the famous Diskobolos, with the head of the Lancelotti version, is due to Professor Rizzo.

[3] As on some vases, the diskobolos wears such a cap.

[4] *Alcamenes, etc.*, p. 61, n. 1.

[5] Pfuhl, *op. cit.* III, Pl. 177, No. 487.

I have long ago[1] dealt with this subject and endeavoured to show (and I hope succeeded in showing) that the κάρη κομόωντες Ἀχαιοί from the Homeric times onwards to the Spartan heroes

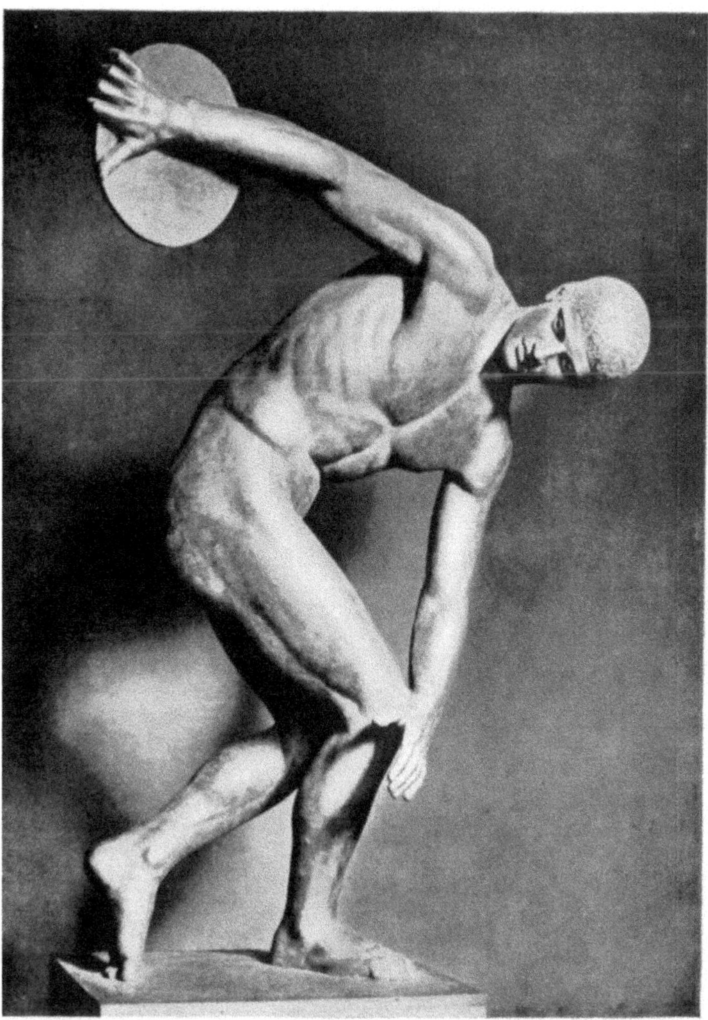

Fig. 4.

of Thermopylae, greatly valued their long hair. No doubt many of the nude figures, hitherto indiscriminately called Apollos, represented nude athletes. This applies even to those who have long

[1] *Pythagoras of Rhegion and the early athletic statues* (*J.H.S.* I, 1880, pp. 168–201 and II, 1881, pp. 332–351); reprinted in *Essays on the Art of Pheidias*, Appendix I.

hair, as the two friends Dermys and Kitylos[1] (Fig. 5) were certainly not Apollos. Both Mr E. Norman Gardiner[2] and Mr W. W. Hyde[3] have expressed their doubts as to the identification of early nude figures with Apollo, though Mr Bliss favours my identification. There are thus several statues and statuettes of undoubted athletes with long hair such as the small Diskobolos bronze in the British

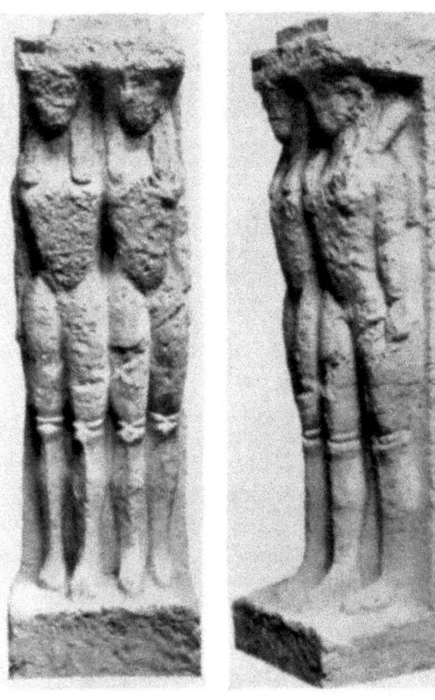

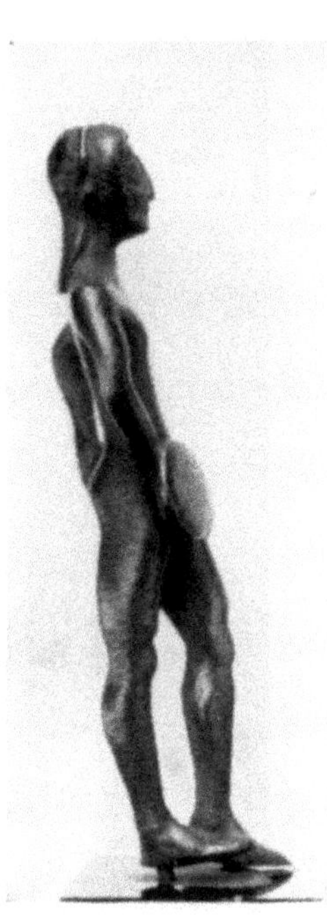

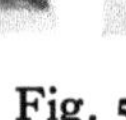

Fig. 5.

Fig. 6.

Museum (Fig. 6), as the Attic Diskophoros slab (Fig. 7)[4] shows the long hair tied together at the end.

If thus even the long-haired nude figures may represent athletes and not Apollos, this applies *a fortiori* to that arrangement of long hair in which it is tightly rolled up at the back and tied or braided round the front. It stands to reason that when long flowing hair

[1] *Gaz. Arch.* 1878, Pl. XXIX; *Ath. Mitt.* III, 1878, Pl. XIV; *Friedr. Woch.* 44.

[2] *Greek Athletic Sports and Festivals*, pp. 88 seq.

[3] *Olympic Victor Monuments and Greek Athletic Art*, pp. 88 seq.

[4] *Alcamenes, etc.*, p. 54, Fig. 56; Brunn-Bruckmann, 475 *b*. Besides the bronze statuette (with hair rolled up in the back) in the Brit. Mus. (No. 675) I have seen a bronze statuette of a nude archaic figure with long hair holding a discus; but I have failed to find it among my notes nor can I exactly remember in what public or private collection I have seen it.

might be an impediment where violent action is taken, especially as in games, some means must be found to reduce it to the most compact form around the head. In the case of warriors wearing a helmet, or without it, we distinctly have this headdress, e.g. in the Aegina Pediments and in the forward striding nude figure

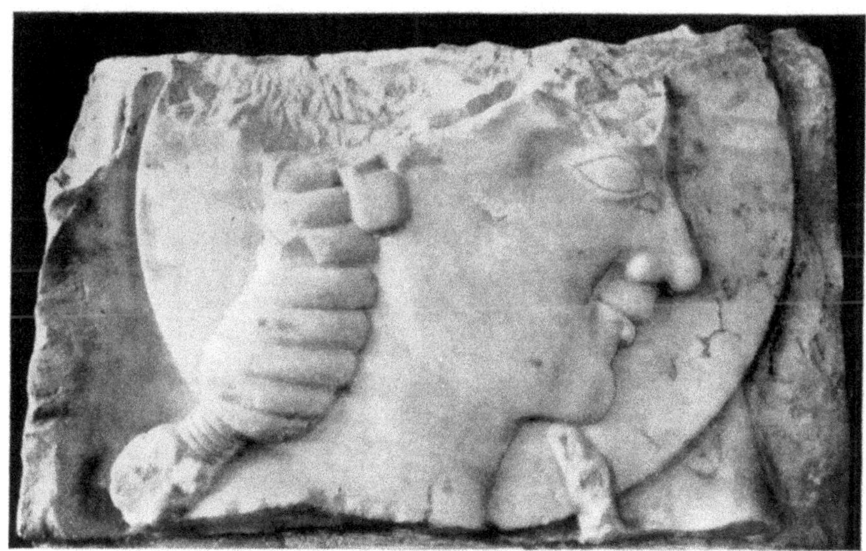

Fig. 7.

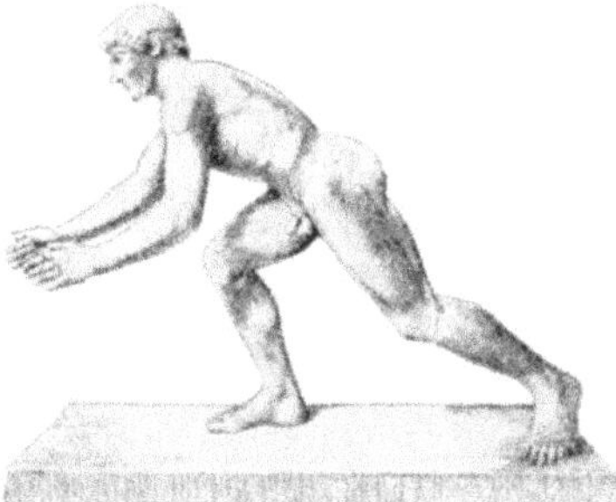

Fig. 8.

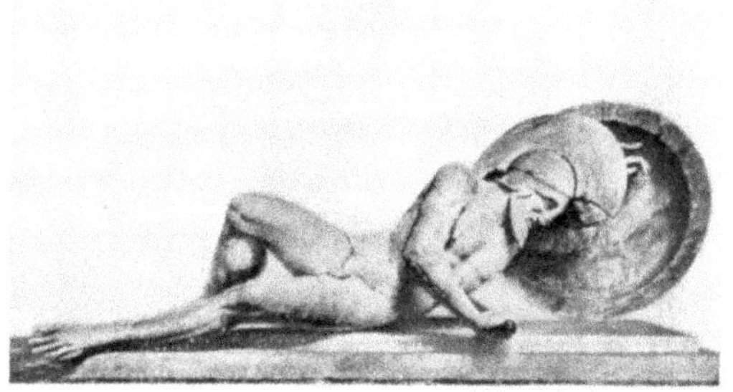

Fig. 9.

without a helmet from that pediment (Fig. 8). The Strangford "Apollo"[1] (Fig. 10) has this arrangement of the hair, as also the Choiseul-Gouffier so-called "Apollo" or pugilist. On practically all the black-figured vases[2] and many of the severer red-figured

[1] *Alcamenes, etc.*, p. 31, Fig. 19.

[2] Cf. Gardiner, *loc. cit.* p. 360, Fig. 107; p. 361, Fig. 108; Leyden vase, *Arch. Zeit.* XXXIX (1881), Pl. IX; Hind, *op. cit.* p. 192, Fig. 36 *a* and *b*; p. 193, Fig. 37; p. 211, Fig. 44.

vases[1] this arrangement of long hair is clearly indicated. A chronological landmark is afforded by coins from Cos of the early part of the fifth century B.C., on which the diskobolos shows the older long

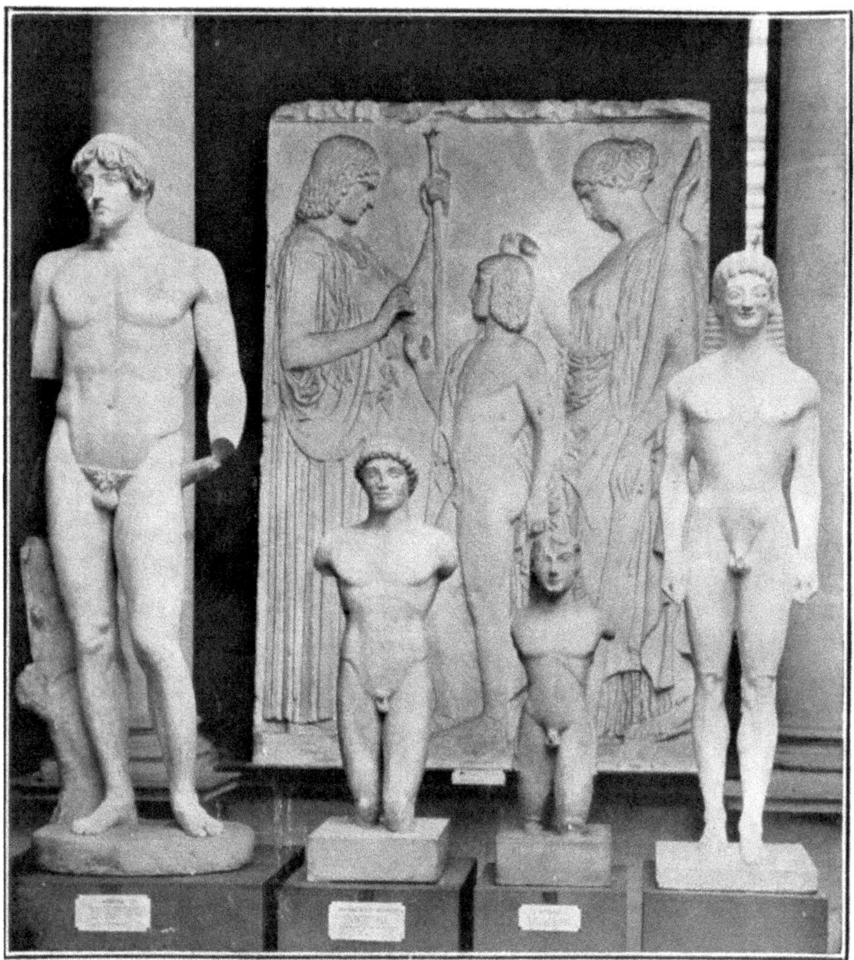

Fig. 10.

hair (Pl. II, fig. 11). The custom or fashion of cutting the hair short must have been introduced during the second quarter of the fifth century B.C. and was certainly established about 450 B.C.; after which boys and ephebi and all athletes have short hair. But

[1] Cf. Gardiner, p. 105, Fig. 17. The *Panaitios Kylix* shows some with long hair, some with cap; p. 305, Fig. 66 (Bourguignon Coll., now in Boston, *Arch. Zeit.* 1884, XVI); p. 323, Fig. 76 (Brit. Mus. E. 6); p. 345, Fig. 96 (psykter, Bourguignon Coll., now in Boston); p. 349, Fig. 100 (Munich 5620); p. 361, Fig. 108. This latter is a vase by Douris (Pottier, *Douris, etc.* (1904), Fig. 6).

PLATE II

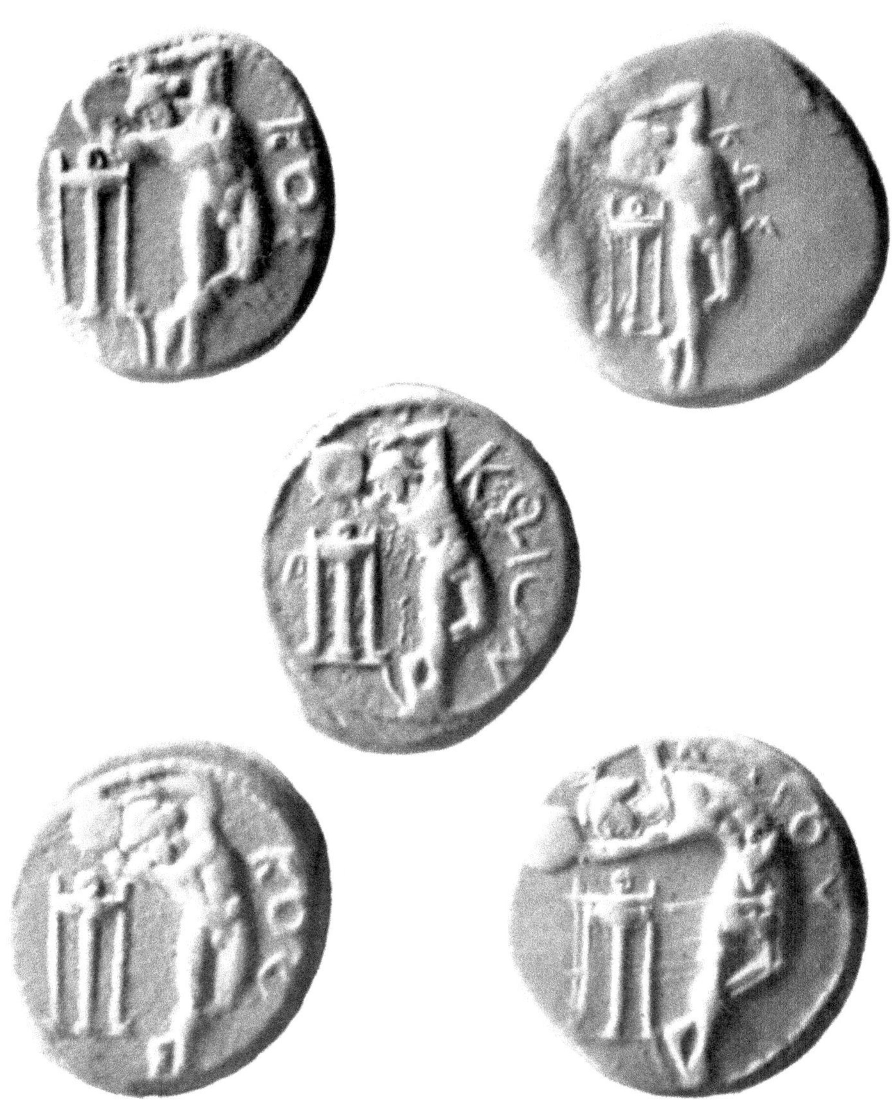

Fig. 11.

in this transitional period we are justified in considering all nude figures with the compact treatment of long hair rolled up around the back of the head and tied or braided in front to be of athletic character.

I therefore again maintain with conviction based upon wide evidence, that types such as the Choiseul-Gouffier "Apollo"

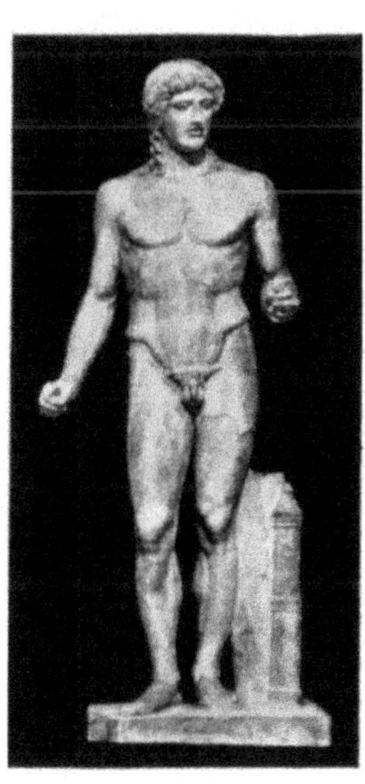

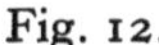

Fig. 12.

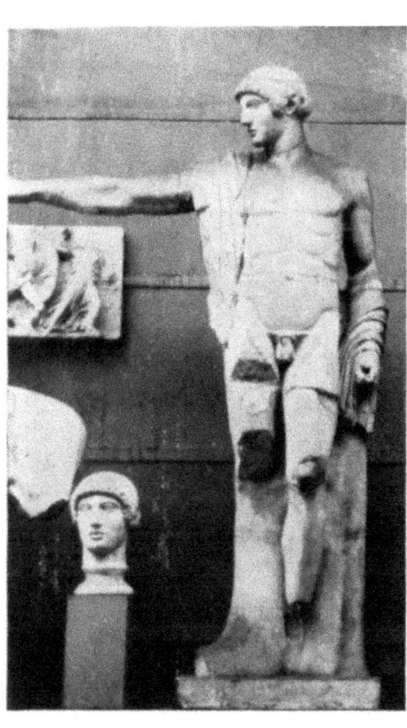

Fig. 13.

(Fig. 15) and the "Apollo" of the Omphalos[1] represent athletes and not Apollos. The god Apollo, as in the case of the Cassel (Fig. 12)[2] and other similar types[3] (which have been ascribed to Phidias) when represented nude and without drapery, have, as the distinctive feature of the god, the long curls hanging down the side, giving a more ornate character to the statue of such a divinity.

[1] I proved long ago (*Pythagoras, etc., loc. cit.*) that the Athenian statue could not have stood on the marble Omphalos.

[2] I here give the reproduction from Miss Margarete Bieber's Catalogue of sculptures of the Museum of Cassel, 1915. This copy of the Apollo is less restored than the later reproduction of that type reproduced by me (*Alcamenes, etc.*, Pl. XXIV) from Michon (*L'Apollon Cherchel*, Mon. et Mém. Acad. des Inscript. xxii (1916)).

[3] *Vide Alcamenes*, Pl. XXIV.

I further emphatically maintain that I was right in identifying the Choiseul-Gouffier and kindred statues with those of a famous victor in the boxing match. The object hanging down the side of the tree-stem could not have served as the strap to a quiver. It is hung round the twig at the top and hangs down straight and is bevelled off at the end as is shown in the accompanying drawing by my daughter (Fig. 17). This was certainly a ἱμάς or leather strap

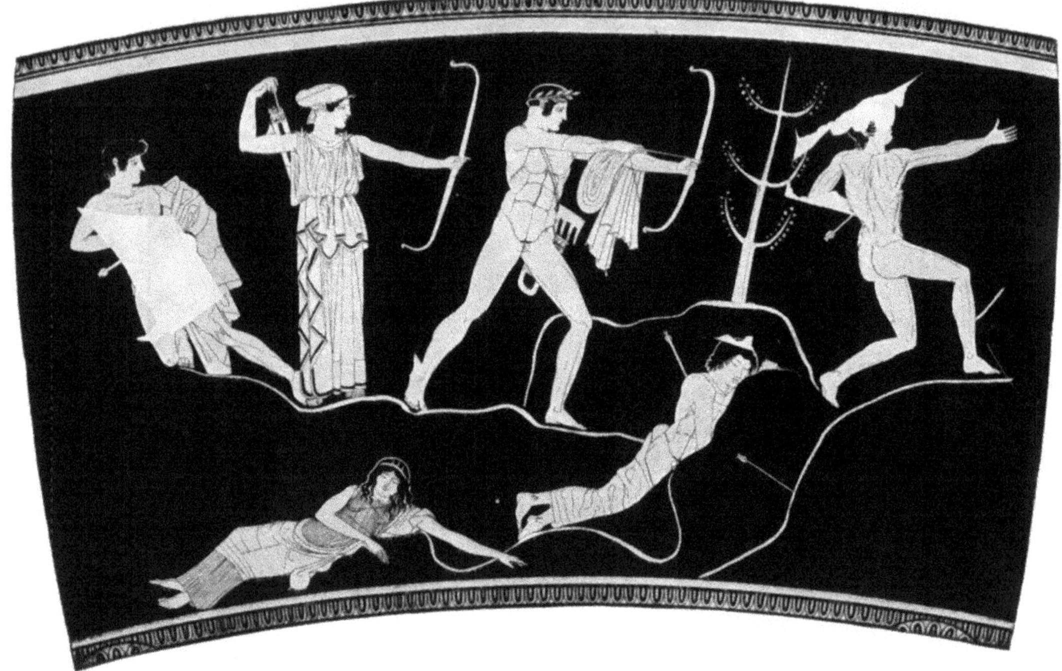

Fig. 14.

which was wound round the fist of the boxer, such as is shown on vases[1], both black-figured and red-figured (Figs. 18 and 19). This object, moreover, is held in the hand of the *ephedros* waiting his turn on the right of the two boxing figures on a black-figured vase in the British Museum, whose attitude, with chest protruding, is that of the Choiseul-Gouffier pugilist[2]. The statue of the pugilist might thus be restored holding the himas in the right hand and

[1] See the black-figured Panathenaic Amphora (Brit. Mus. B. 140—there appears to exist a replica of this vase at Philadelphia (Hyde, *op. cit.* p. 242, Fig. 56)). See also the red-figured vase, *J.H.S.* XXVI (1906), Pl. XII.

[2] *J.H.S.* II (1881), p. 340, Fig. 2; *Art of Pheidias*, p. 360, Fig. 21.

the end of which hangs over the tree-stem, bevelled off at end (Figs. 16 and 17), and possibly the victor's wreath or an olive twig in the upraised left hand with bent arm. Now, this attitude corresponds to that on a coin from Pandosia in Bruttium[1] with, on the obverse, a female head with inscription surrounded by a laurel wreath and, on the reverse, the figure of a nude youth holding in his right hand a patera or a wreath and in his left hand a laurel branch[2].

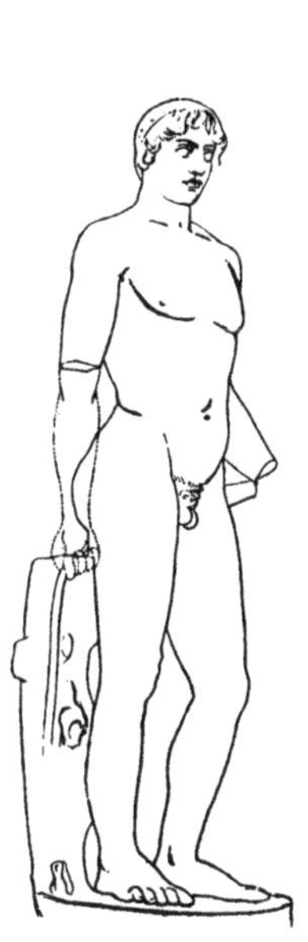

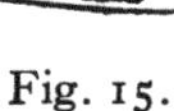

Fig. 15.

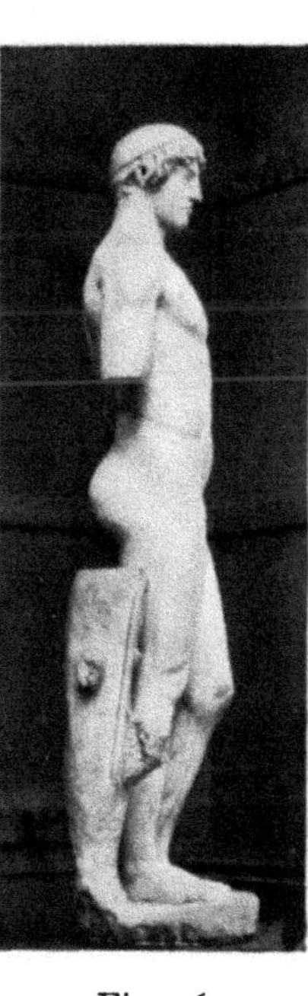

Fig. 16.

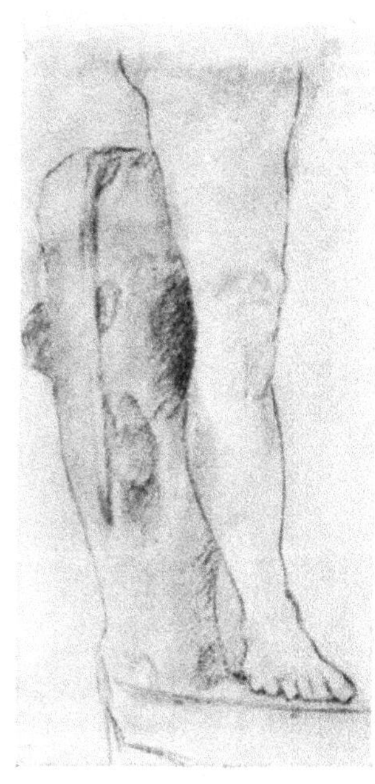

Fig. 17.

But still more striking is the figure of the nude youth on the coin from Selinus (Fig. 20)[3], which corresponds markedly to that of the Choiseul-Gouffier pugilist in attitude, proportion, indication of muscles, even down to the headdress. Moreover, I give, side by side (Fig. 20)[4], the so-called Apollo on the Omphalos and the Naples Doryphoros of Polykleitos, below which are placed the coin

[1] Cf. my article in *J.H.S.* II, 1881, p. 348, Fig. 4.

[2] I must here urgently recommend that my two articles in *J.H.S.* of 1880 and 1881, reprinted in the Appendix to my *Art of Pheidias*, be carefully reconsidered. It is there shown how famous athletes like Euthymos, Theagenes and Kleomedes became heroes and were worshipped. The statue of the pugilist Euthymos by Pythagoras was most famous. Moreover river gods (like Krathis on the coin of Pandosia) when youthful were given athletic forms.

[3] *Ibid.* p. 348, Fig. 4.

[4] Reproduced from my article in *Essays on the Art of Pheidias*, Appendix I, p. 371, Fig. 23.

of Selinus dating *circ.* the middle of the fifth century B.C. and the same coin about the end of the fifth century B.C. On comparing these figures it will be seen that the type of the pugilist on the

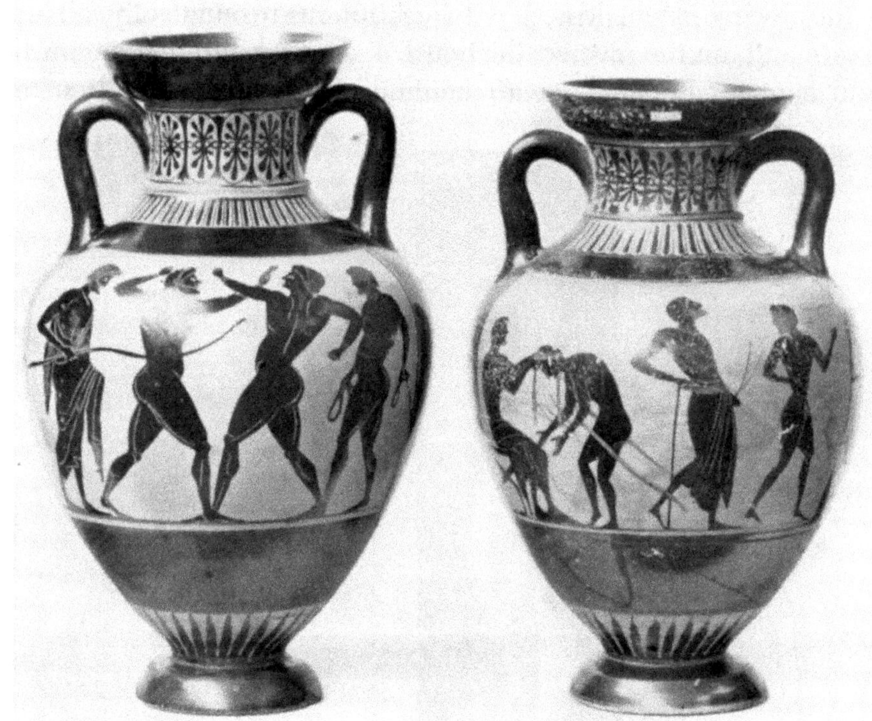

Fig. 18.

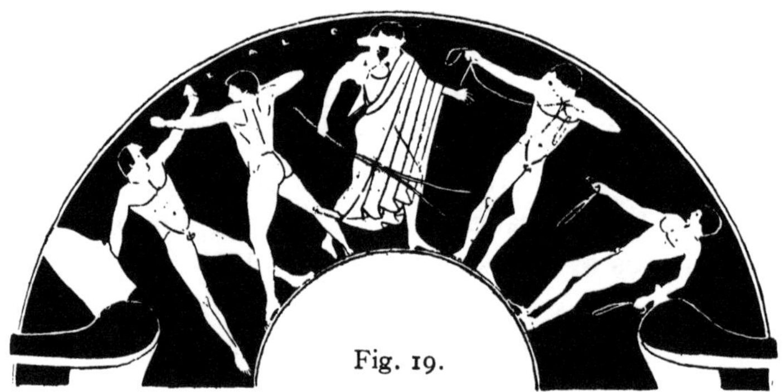

Fig. 19.

earlier coin of Selinus, corresponding to the statue of the pugilist, changes to the heavier and squatter proportions of the figure placed above the coin, the head becoming larger and more rectangular, and the attitude that of walking, corresponding (as much as a small coin can do) to the change as effected in the Doryphoros, the Polykleitan canon. When we bear in mind the fact that the coins of Magna Graecia and Sicily thus reproduce the type established in the first half of the fifth century B.C. by Pythagoras in his famous athlete statues, that of the pugilist Euthymos being one of the most famous of his works, the hypothesis that the Choiseul-Gouffier and similar statues of pugilists reproduce the famous works of that eminent sculptor from Rhegium, is most completely justified. Let us hope that some day further excavations carried on in Sicily and in the flourishing cities of Magna Graecia such as Sybaris, Kroton, Rhegion, etc. may produce final evidence in finds bearing upon this hypothesis. Meanwhile, I emphatically maintain that there is more probability in favour of my hypothetical identification than in that which considers these statues to be reproductions of the Apollo by the Attic sculptor Kalamis, whose grace and softness were characteristics specially mentioned by Lucian and other authors with regard to his Sosandra, and who, in spite of his proficiency in rendering horses (*equis semper sine aemulo expressis*—Plin. *N.H.* XXXIV, 71), was never noted for athletic statues. This ancient "Pre-Raphaelite" artist of the Transition Period was chiefly noted for the quaint grace and softness of his works, not for athletic vigour. Lucian (*Imagg.* 6) praises in the Sosandra τὸ μειδίαμα σεμνὸν καὶ λεληθός, while Quintilian (*Inst. Orat.* XII, 10, 7) considered him less hard in style than Kallon and Hegesias.

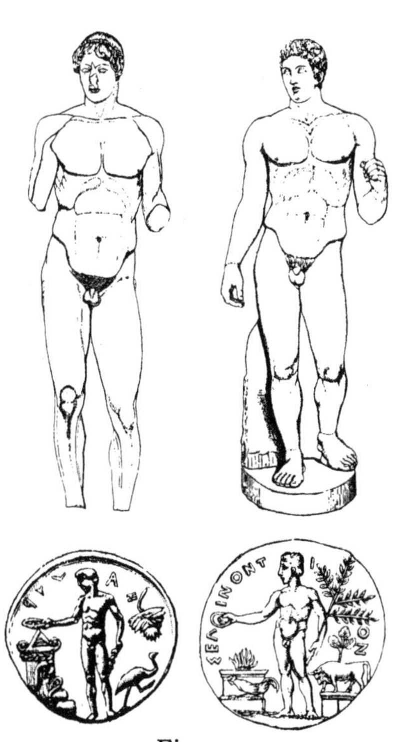

Fig. 20.

On the other hand, when the Apollo himself is shown in a distinctly athletic action or surroundings (as, for instance, in the Western Pediment of Olympia) (Fig. 13), or in warlike action (as on the Niobe vase (Fig. 14), where he advances slaying with his arrows) he is then represented as an athlete or a warrior. These vases show the god Apollo and the heroes Theseus and Peirithoös in such warlike and athletic poses, with the "athletic" arrangement of the hair in that earlier period.

In fine, I still maintain that merely as a hypothesis (and in such identifications it is only a question of probability, not of certainty) these latter reproductions of an earlier bronze illustrate to us what the famous statue of Euthymos by Pythagoras was like.

There can be no doubt that the prominent sculptors of athletic art in the first half of the fifth century B.C. had the greatest influence in establishing types, especially of the body, which gave the lasting eminence to the classical type for all ages. I endeavoured over forty years ago[1] (and since then in Chapters III, IV, V of *Alcamenes, etc.*) to demonstrate the great influence which in general the palaestra had upon Greek art. I even then maintained, as I do now, that the ancient Greeks were the only people who developed athletic exercises and games for their own sake, as they also were the only people of antiquity who produced the *statue* and the *picture* as such, to satisfy the aesthetic demands of the human mind independently of the purely decorative or religiously ancillary function of art in all other countries of the ancient world. These two achievements are not accidental, but are essentially interwoven with one another and, together with the development of pure science or philosophy, formed the leading characteristics of Hellenism. I am glad to find that, since then, Professor Furtwängler (*Die Bedeutung der Gymnastik in der Griechischen Kunst*), Mr E. Norman Gardiner and Mr W. W. Hyde, in their general works on Greek athletics, have admitted this supreme influence of the palaestra on Greek art and have contributed to confirm my own early exposition of that important question. I am also gratified to find that the supreme importance of Pythagoras, which I endeavoured to prove in my early papers, has been recognised in several separate monographs and articles on that ancient sculptor; but I regret to find that, both as regards the undeniable athletic type in the Choiseul-Gouffier and the Athenian statues, in contradistinction to the type of Apollo, as well as my identification of these works with such a statue by Pythagoras, have not been accepted by several of my colleagues, perhaps with the exception of the late Professor Overbeck.

[1] *The Influence of Athletic Games upon Greek Art* (*Proceedings of the Royal Institution* 1883); *Essays on the Art of Pheidias*, Appendix III, p. 394.

II

A MARBLE DRAPED FEMALE FIGURE IN BURLINGTON HOUSE

THE beautiful marble torso of a draped female figure in the official apartments of the Royal Academicians—"the Saloon" of Burlington House—attracted my attention[1] some considerable time ago, as being a remarkable specimen of Greek sculpture of the best period of Greek art, probably of the last quarter of the fifth century B.C. down to the middle of the fourth century B.C. About two years ago I procured the authority of the President and Council of the Royal Academy to publish this important work. This publication has necessarily been delayed for some time. Not only does it seem to me most desirable that some reproduction should be in the hands of my colleagues here and abroad and should be brought to the cognisance of those in charge of excavations and museums, so that its origin and original destination should be definitely ascertained; but I have been informed recently that a younger archaeologist is desirous of publishing it in some art magazine, to which, as far as I am concerned, I saw no objection. It was my intention to delay publication until after a visit to certain ancient sites or museums (including parts of Italy and Greece). But it is fairer and wiser to publish adequate illustrations (Pl. III) at once, so that foreign colleagues can co-operate in throwing light on this interesting fragment.

As to its *provenance*, nothing is known. Mr Lamb has kindly searched all documents and records of the Royal Academy[2], but no information as to the donor, the date of its donation, or its origin in the ancient world is forthcoming. It seems to me not impossible that it may have been presented by the architect Cockerell. I have generally been able to distinguish *macroscopically*

[1] It was my wife who first drew my attention to it.

[2] Since this paper was read on February 8, a letter from Mr G. Clausen, R.A., in the *Times* (a notice was published in its columns on February 9) informs us that "the very beautiful statue had been given to the Academy by Henry Weekes, the sculptor. It was then in the schools, in one of the class-rooms, but was removed to its present position about 12 years ago, to avoid risk of injury."

between Pentelic and Parian marble from the respective nature of the surface-patina. But this marble has no doubt been, in the past, subjected to various methods of cleaning, which has materially affected the antique surface.

The figure is of Greek marble, neither Italian nor modern. The head and neck are missing, as well as both feet, the right arm and hand below the middle of the biceps, the left wrist and hand; while smaller portions of the drapery—extremities of folds and the upper part of the right breast—are broken away. Otherwise this draped female torso is in perfect preservation.

There are no restorations, excepting that a triangular wedge of hard composite has been inserted between the two ankles, so that the figure should remain in its upright position on its pedestal.

This upright attitude is slightly modified in that, as will be seen in the side view (Pl. III, fig. 22), the upper part of the body leans slightly forward. No doubt the head and neck were also thus bent forward, the head probably also downward and towards our left. We cannot now determine the action of the hands and what was held in them. The left knee is bent slightly forward, while the right is pressed back, though slightly flexed and not in a position indicative of complete rest and repose. Though the neck and head were turned towards the left arm, the upper part of the body, as is seen from the exact position of the breast, was slightly turned towards our right. The right breast is completely uncovered, the drapery having slipped down from the left shoulder in a heavy mass of folds, which almost suggests that the drapery was damped. The undergarment clings to the body in softer masses of folds, but the delicate ridges of these folds are firmly cut in sharp, though very slight, ridges, widening out into one mass of relief in more varied masses and curves where they are crushed by the heavier mass of horizontal folds of the thicker upper garment, when this passes from one side over the middle of the figure and over the projecting left arm and waist. From the breasts downwards, as well as over the legs, the nude forms shine through clearly, the delicate folds and texture of the undergarment being firmly carved. The folds of the upper-garment on either side and between the legs are indicated still more boldly and with undercutting, and show, in the frontal view, especially on *our* right side, forward movement of the figure or the effect of wind. On our left side, however (Pl. III, fig. 22), these deeper folds are

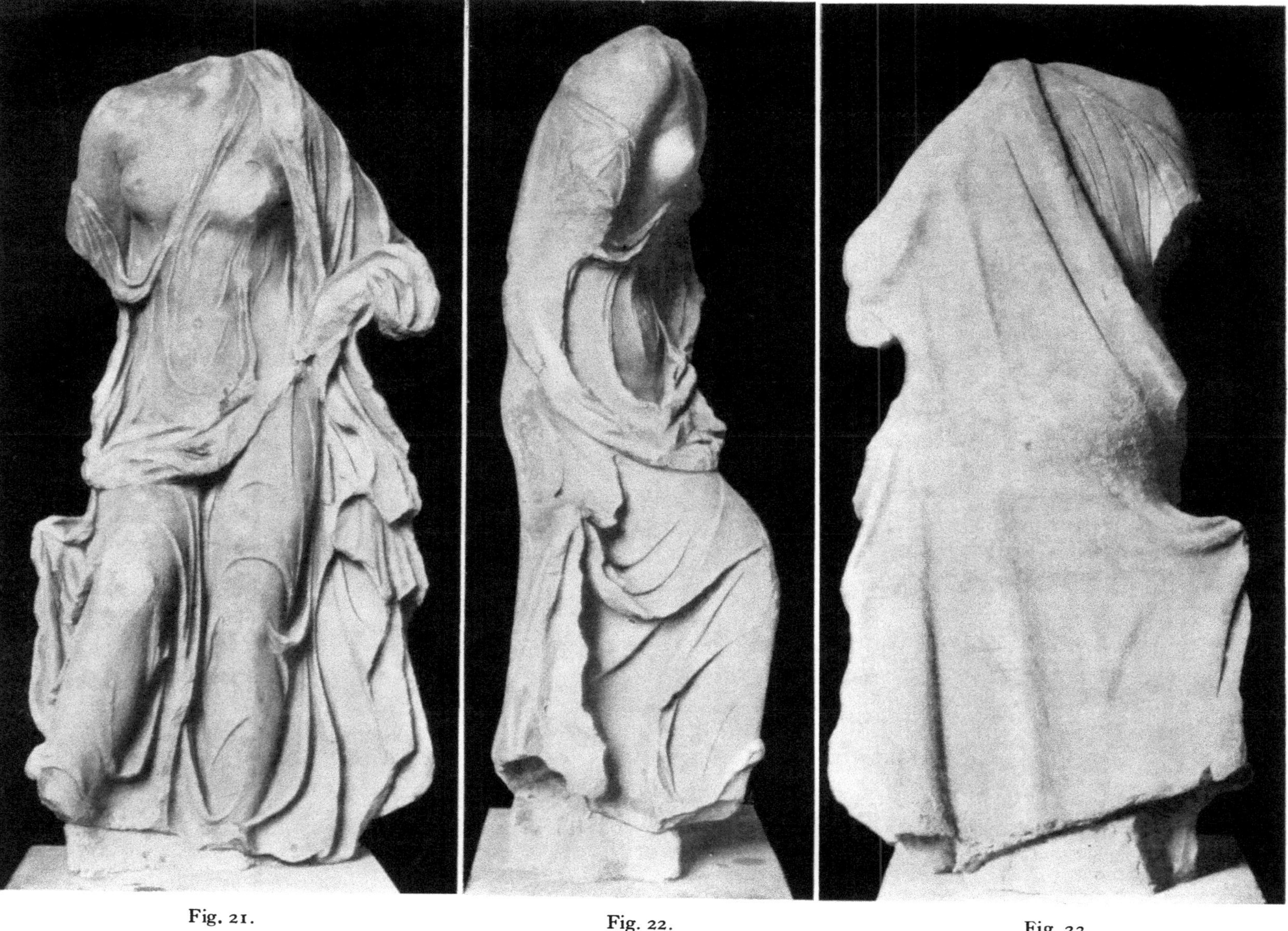

Fig. 21.

Fig. 22.

Fig. 23.

heavy in their tension and show perhaps similar moistening of the drapery as we noticed it in the folds of the undergarment below the right breast. It is not unlikely that the extended right arm of the figure held the end of the drapery in the right hand.

At first sight the beautiful relief of the Sandal-binding Victory from the balustrade of the temple of the Nike Apteros at once suggests itself (Fig. 24). Here we certainly have the rendering of the *tralucida veste pinxit* first ascribed to Polygnotos and illustrated in many Attic vases and, from the Parthenon sculptures onward, in Attic sculpture. But in our figure occasional heaviness in the material may suggest the clinging quality of moistened drapery.

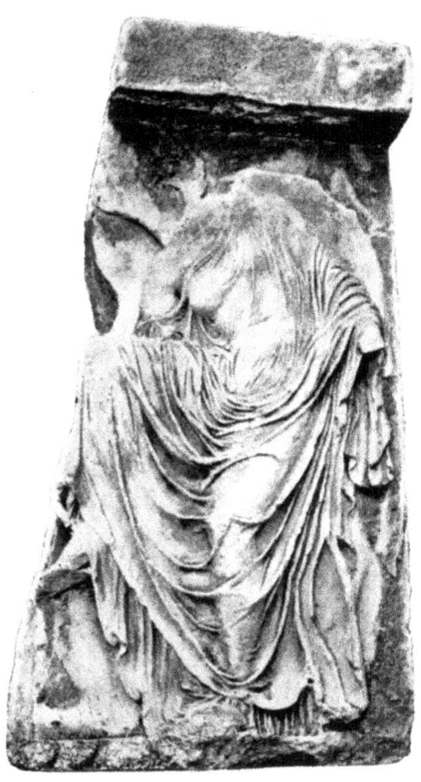

Fig. 24.

Moreover, the dimensions of the figures (about half life-size) in the Nike of the balustrade and our figure are about the same. Greatest height (without head and neck) about 2 ft. 7 in. or 78·5 cm. in our marble and about the same in the Nike. The thickness of the balustrade, according to Mr Casson[1], is 23 cm., while the greatest thickness in our figure is *circ.* 23·5 cm. The reliefs in the balustrade are often completely undercut, but are, at least in some part, joined on to the background.

Now, the back of our figure (Pl. III, fig. 23) is nowhere attached to a background. The figure was therefore completely worked in the round and could not have formed part of a frieze in relief, however much it was undercut. On the other hand, it was meant to be seen

[1] *Catalogue of the Acropolis Museum*, II, p. 15. For the sculptures of that temple besides the earlier work of Kekulé, see Heberdey, in the *Jahreshefte* (*Wien*), XIII (1910) and XXI–XXII, 1–82 (1922–24); also C. Blumel, *Der Fries des Tempels der Athena Nike*, Berlin, 1923, where other literature is given.

only from the front or on the sides, not from the back, as will be evident when we note the summary and flat treatment of the back (Pl. III, fig. 23). It therefore formed part of a group in a shallow pediment of smaller dimensions or some single figure fitting in with an architectural arrangement. It would thus correspond most to one of the Nereids[1] placed between the columns of the Nereid-Tomb from Xanthos in the British Museum, which the moist and clinging quality of the drapery also suggests. Among the several Nereids, most of which were probably placed between the pillars of the peristyle, one, No. 909 (Fig. 26), approaches in style to the Burlington House figure; but the dimensions are slightly larger, while these Nereids were also seen from the back, which is finished in workmanship. But the figure of a girl in flowing and clinging drapery (Fig. 25 *a*, *b*, *c*), No. 919 in the catalogue[2], was not intended to be seen from the back which is not completely finished and is kept quite flat (Fig. 25 *b*). It may therefore have been placed beside the door leading from the colonnade into the chamber. The dimensions of this Nereid, moreover, correspond to those of our statue. From about the ankle to the beginning of the neck is *circ.* 35 in. (89 cm.) as compared with 31 in. (78·5 cm.) in our figure. The greatest thickness, 9½ in., is almost the same (23·5 cm.) in our figure. Both figures might thus have been placed beside the door or, possibly, might have surmounted the roof with the acroteria.

Some analogies in style can also be found in some of the sculptures from the Erechtheum at Athens[3], those of Asklepios at Epidaurus[4], with the frieze representing the Wedding of Poseidon and Amphitrite at Munich[5]. I should not be inclined to assign it to the Neo-Attic School or the first century of Imperial Rome. We cannot go far wrong in fixing its date between the years 430 B.C. and 350 B.C.

[1] *Brit. Mus. Cat.* See also Niemann, *Das Nereiden Monument, etc.* Wien, 1921. See also F. Krischen, *Mitth. Athen.* XXXVIII (1923), who gives a later date (*circ.* 375 B.C.) to this monument; but Bruno Schröder subsequently returns to the earlier dating in the fifth century B.C.

[2] A. H. Smith, *Cat. of Sculp. Brit. Mus.* II, 37.

[3] On the Erechtheum, see Holland, Dinsmoor and others, *Amer. Jour. Arch.* XXVIII, 1924 and 1926. Earlier work, such as that of Kekulé, is there quoted.

[4] Kavvadias, *Epidaure*, Pl. IX.

[5] See also Carl Blümel, *Der Fries des Tempels der Athena Nike* (Berlin, 1923); Heberdey, *Die Komposition der Reliefs an der Balustrade der Athena Nike* (*Jahreshefte d. Arch. Inst., Wien*, XXI–XXII, 1922–24).

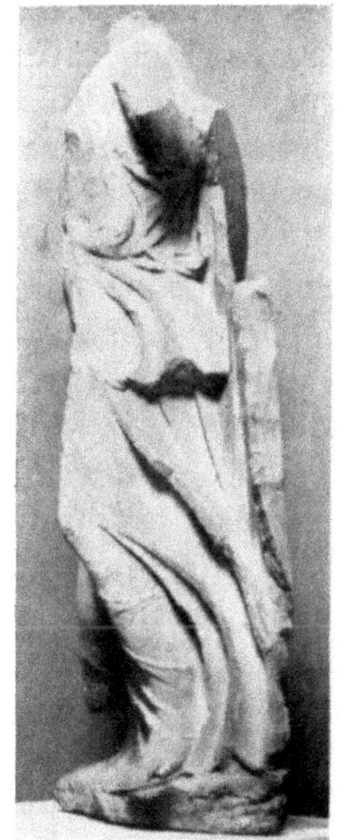

Fig. 25 *a*.

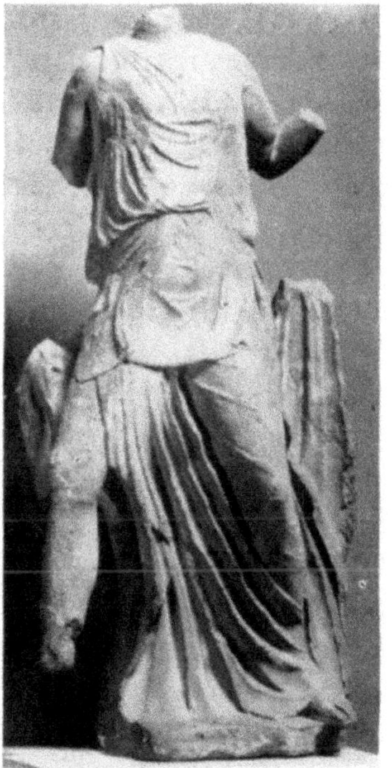

Fig. 25 *b*.

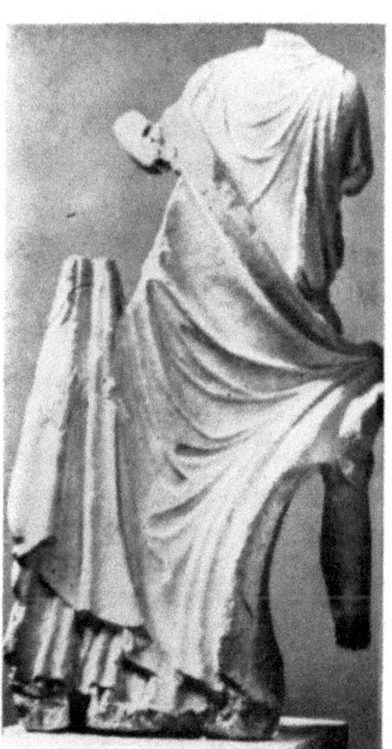

Fig. 25 *c*.

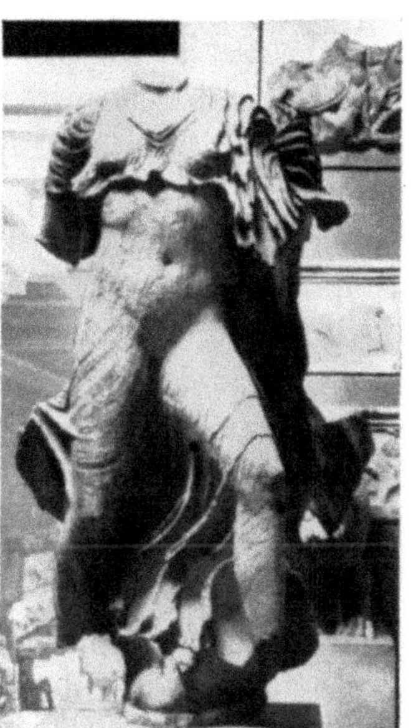

Fig. 26.

On pp. 111 seq. and pp. 245 to 246 of my *Alcamenes, etc.* I point out how, in the Parthenon, the modelling and carving of drapery, especially in the female figures from the Eastern Pediment, was carried to a high state of perfection. Not only in Attica, but also in the works of other schools in the second half of the fifth century B.C., do we perceive the influence of this advance in treatment of drapery. This is especially the case in the balustrade of the Nike temple with some further steps in definite elaboration of drapery and folds. But we may even look further back than the Parthenon sculptures to the painter Polygnotos, who, we learn from Pliny[1], *primus mulieres tralucida veste pinxit*, and probably through whom many of the Attic vase-painters, influenced by him, made considerable advance in the indication of delicate texture and folds in female drapery. This especially shows itself in what might be called the *linear* indication of such folds, which naturally and readily would also influence the sculptors in similar works. Though in the next generation such delicate line and outline drawing was, no doubt, carried to still further perfection by such a painter as Parrhasios, the development of pictorial art in ancient Greece, from Apollodoros onwards[2], led more and more to the indication of modelling and texture by means of light and shade and the mixing of colours (in contradistinction to the *simplex color* of their old masters), which, again, led to the establishment of colour-values. Thus, with the direct influence of scene-painting, *skiagraphia* (σκιαγραφία) and *skenographia* (σκηνογραφία) together led in the fourth century to broader treatment of pictorial effects in drapery, reacting upon sculpture in the indication of texture; until, finally, in the later centuries, the more minute linear folding again asserted itself in more elaborate clinging and almost damped drapery.

We thus find, towards the close of the fifth century B.C., remarkable technical skill in the rendering of texture in drapery, of which the Sandal-binding Nike from the balustrade of the temple of Nike Apteros gives us so full an illustration, and it is to these and the immediately following years, from *circ.* 430 to 350 B.C.[3], that we should assign the Burlington House marble.

[1] *N. H.* xxxv, 58.

[2] See Overbeck, *Schriftquellen, etc.*, 1641–1646.

[3] I have just seen a paper on the well-known statue of the Nike of Samothrace in the Louvre and kindred statues by Mr A. W. Lawrence, in the current (January 28,

1927) number of the *Journal of Hellenic Studies*. The paper is careful, suggestive and instructive. I am especially struck by his analogy to ancient art in the later developments of the "Barocco" style and of Canova's classicism in modern art. But the article does not deal with the important problem of the treatment of drapery in the sculpture of the fifth century B.C., from the female figures in the Parthenon sculptures, followed by those of Phigalia, the Argive Heraeum, the Erechtheum, the temple of Athena Nike at Athens down to the earlier works of the fourth century B.C. associated with Timotheos and the draped figures of Epidaurus. These all present the crucial question of the treatment of drapery in Greek Art.

For EU product safety concerns, contact us at Calle de José Abascal, 56–1°, 28003 Madrid, Spain or eugpsr@cambridge.org.

www.ingramcontent.com/pod-product-compliance
Ingram Content Group UK Ltd.
Pitfield, Milton Keynes, MK11 3LW, UK
UKHW050731090726
473066UK00013B/1108

* 9 7 8 1 1 0 7 6 6 3 6 2 6 *